loveamore

Copyright © 1989 by Esme Kent

Copyright © 2021 by loveamore pty ltd

All rights reserved. No part of this book may be reproduced in any manner whatsoever without written permission except in the case of brief quotations embodied in critical articles and reviews.

First produced, 1989 as a self-published printed pamphlet.

First published, 2021.

This is the story of CY O'Connor and his amazing engineering accomplishment which provided a water supply to the Goldfields.

First produced as a self-published pamphlet by Esme and her husband David in 1989, the story was sold in the Kalgoorlie tourist bureau, the couple shared all profits with the Royal Flying Doctors.

The pamphlet was illustrated in 1989 in pen and ink by Derek Kent, a renowned Australian artist.

THE STORY OF CY O'CONNOR

By Esme Kent

Illustrations by Derek Kent

loveamore

The long grey pipe,

weaves its dusty way, from the city to the outback, 600 kilometres away.

Pumping fresh, clean water, through the bush and sand, bringing civilisation,

to a dry desert land.

It was John Forrest and CY O'Connor,

who first thought of the idea, of transporting water, from Mundaring Weir. Yet people shook their heads, saying it's bound to be a flop, pipes need joints and rivets, and they will rust and rot.

Thirty-one plans were drawn,

from them chosen three, blueprints of a scheme,

to build a pipe to Kalgoorlie.

O'Connor the driving force, knew it could be done, with the help of a colleague, Mephan Ferguson.

They invented a locking bar,

pressure squeezed and fused, more reliable than riveted pipes,

which previously were used. Then 28 foot length cylinders, were firmly clamped together, making water tight compartments,

as protection from the weather.

Work began in April,
in 1898,
cutting through the bush,
at a slow and steady rate.
Then came delays,
and frustrations many,
"We can't afford it", cried the Politicians,
"We won't give another penny".

CY O'Connor became a target,

the crowd were an angry mob, they didn't think he could do, this extraordinary job.

They fought and raged against him, it would make any faint heart quail,

yet O'Connor quietly worked on,

convinced he wouldn't fail.

This vast project,

took five years to complete, until rivers of pure water, flowed to the bottom of Hannan Street.

Bright lights played on fountains,

reservoirs were lit up, and a blackened billy can, was used as the first cup.

Temperatures were high,

over 42 degrees in the shade, it didn't bother anyone, because history had been made.

Celebrations went wild,

the people had a roaring time, as sprinklers were turned on everywhere,

from that famous grey pipeline.

A modern city flourished,

at the end of that dusty pipe, people came in droves,

*of each and every type.
Tons more gold was mined, out of the rich, red earth, now the luxury of water, had given the town new birth.*

So, gold brought the water,

and water brought the green, new grass and flowers grew, where hard baked soil had been.

Colourful parks and gardens, emerged from the landscape bare, as tall trees by the score, were planted everywhere.

Unhappily O'Connor,

never lived to see,

the fruits of his efforts, that transformed Kalgoorlie. Just a short time earlier, he died by his own hand, the man whose dream brought water,

to a dry, desert land.

MR C. Y. O'CONNOR,
C.M.G., M.I.C.E.
(LATE ENGINEER-IN-CHIEF FOR
WESTERN AUSTRALIA)

About the Author

Esme has some wonderful stories to tell, from her days as a causality evacuation medic with the Royal Air Force to running boarding schools in outback Australia.

An active community member, volunteering as the first female to go on a live rescue in the wild Irish seas to dedicating years as a crisis telephone counsellor and Justice of the Peace.

Writing articles for local papers as well as writing historical ballads, children's stories and poems

Esme achieved a black belt in Karate when she was 58 years young and she went on to walk the Bibulmum track from end to end when she was 60 and for her 70th birthday became a pilgrim walking the Camino de Santiago trial in Spain.

Esme has delved into many writing genres, even doing a stint teaching creative writing in Esperance, Western Australia.

Esme celebrated her 54th wedding anniversary recently and has two daughters and a grandson.

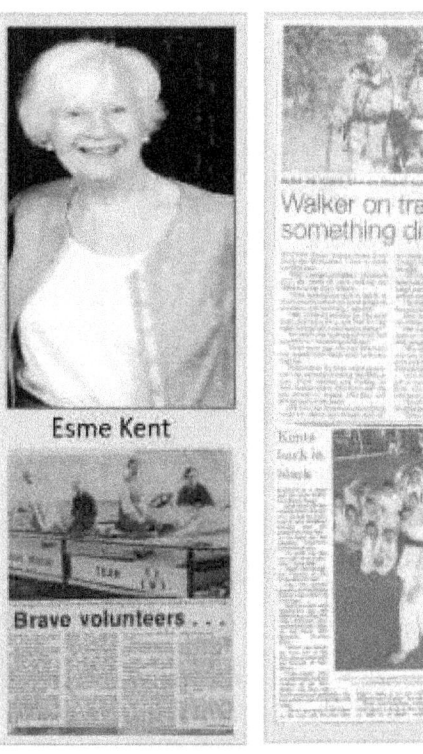

About the Illustrator

Derek was born and educated in England. He studied at Bromley College of arts in England and was in the printing industry for 34 years. His skills as a printer helped in his development of illustrations in black and white and used the subtle dyes of his trade for shading effects. He developed a steady hand after years of training as a colour re-toucher.

Whilst living in England he commenced studies in oil painting. On immigrating to South Africa in 1971 he further developed his black and white pen drawings seeking out the South African scenes.

He became aware of the deeper richer colours of Africa and his oil paintings took on the brilliant colours all around him. He had successful exhibitions in Durban and local art shows. He spent many hours studying the sea and seascapes were to become his favourite subject.

In 1980 he immigrated to Melbourne. Australia. He joined the Australian Guild of Realist Artists in 1988 and it was through attending many workshops he was able to absorb the intriguing methods used in watercolour. Derek went on to produce many water colours one of which received a highly commended at a rotary exhibition held in Melbourne and was subsequently sold.

Loveamore Other titles

Esme Kent has provided a fresh feel to motivation and inspiration with her book of sayings and quotes you can use to bring fresh perspectives to your day, to a situation or to a lift your spirits and provide that extra bounce in your step. In finding a new perspective, a different way of sharing a thought, a new outlook, an open mind, an inspired heart Esme has provided a path to finding re-invention in ourselves, finding magic, and ultimately weaving magic into our lives.

A collection of poems from the soul for the soul, may words bring to life memories, feelings and emotions that move you, inspire you, ignite you as many moments have inspired this collection. With wonder we walk through the world, with sadness we see its pain, with joy we experience its beauty., with hope you will find beauty and inspiration in these words, from my heart to yours with love, peace and blessings.

Bonnie is a beautiful and loveable dog, she loves to say hello to people and she has many adventures meeting many new friends when she is out and about on her walks. Join Bonnie on her adventures meeting various animals showing the amazing wildlife you can see while just out walking in the suburbs of Quinns Rocks, Butler, Jindalee, Yanchep and Two Rocks in the State of Western Australia. The book uses real life photographs of Bonnie the dog meeting different animals, it is a fun story giving clues to each animal so the reader can guess what they are from the picture and verse.

loveamore Instagram

Socials

Follow loveamore for news of upcoming releases.

loveamore Facebook

www.ingramcontent.com/pod-product-compliance
Lightning Source LLC
Chambersburg PA
CBHW031352160426
42811CB00092B/13